An Invitation to Prayer for Mothers

is a special gift for:

_____

From:

_____

Date:

_____

May you have many defining
moments with God . . .

An
Invitation
to Prayer
for Mothers

by Jack Countryman

THOMAS NELSON
Since 1798

NASHVILLE   DALLAS   MEXICO CITY   RIO DE JANEIRO

Published in Nashville, Tennessee, by Thomas Nelson. Thomas Nelson is a registered trademark of Thomas Nelson, Inc.

Thomas Nelson, Inc. titles may be purchased in bulk for educational, business, fund-raising, or sales promotional use. For information, please e-mail SpecialMarkets@ThomasNelson.com.

All Scripture references are from The NEW KING JAMES VERSION (NKJV). © 1982 by Thomas Nelson, Inc. Used by permission. All rights reserved.

ISBN-13: 978-1-4041-8776-4

Printed in China

09 10 11 12 [TIMS] 5 4 3 2 1

CONTENTS

PREFACE

An Invitation to Prayer for Mothers will draw you closer to the heavenly Father and encourage your heart. Prayer is one of the essential tools the Lord grants to all of us to reveal His will, calm our hearts, and equip us in our daily living and parenting.

Each mother celebrates great joys in life as well as facing challenges of every kind and size. Philippians 4:6 encourages us to pray about everything. So whether you are the mother of a small child, the mother of adult children, the spiritual mother to a new believer, or a mentor to other women, the prayers and Scriptures in this book will help you grow closer to God and experience the fullness of motherhood that God ordained for you and those you love.

In each entry, you will find a focus word, a related Scripture verse, and a prayer to lead you in your time with the Lord. May God lead, guide, and affirm you in your calling of motherhood.

— *Marsha Countryman*

WIFE, MOTHER, GRANDMOTHER, MENTOR

ABILITY

*If anyone speaks, let him speak as the
oracles of God. If anyone ministers, let him
do it as with the ability which God supplies,
that in all things God may be glorified
through Jesus Christ, to whom belong the
glory and the dominion forever and ever.
Amen.*

—1 PETER 4:11

Lord, You have graciously given me certain abilities. May I always be faithful and responsible to live in such a way that You would be honored and glorified. Speak to my heart and may Your Spirit forever guide my thoughts. Help me as a mother to use the gifts You have given me in ways that are pleasing to You. This I ask in Your precious name. Amen.

ABSTAIN

Beloved, I beg you as sojourners and pilgrims, abstain from fleshly lusts which war against the soul, having your conduct honorable among the Gentiles, that when they speak against you as evildoers, they may, by your good works which they observe, glorify God in the day of visitation.

—1 PETER 2:11–12

Father, may You forever be praised. Help me abstain from anything that would take me away from You. Fill me with Your presence and help me be a living example of Your love, grace, and mercy. May my life be a reflection of Your faithfulness. Protect my thoughts and hold me in Your arms for You are my strength and my Redeemer. This I ask in Your most holy name. Amen.

ABUNDANT

Rejoice the soul of Your servant,
For to You, O Lord, I lift up my soul.
For You, Lord, are good, and ready to forgive,
And abundant in mercy to all those
who call upon You.

—PSALM 86:4–5

Oh Father, how wonderful You are. Your love is endless, and Your abundant mercy is new every morning. My heart is filled with praise for Your lovingkindness. Help me as a mother to share Your abundant love with each of my children. May Your Spirit give me the wisdom necessary to guide the precious gifts You have given me. I confess that I cannot live without You in my life. Give me the power of Your presence to live each day for You, my Lord and my Savior. I ask these things in Your most holy name. Amen.

ACCEPTABLE

For you were once darkness,
but now you are light in the Lord.
Walk as children of light
(for the fruit of the Spirit
is in all goodness, righteousness, and truth),
finding out what is acceptable to the Lord.

—EPHESIANS 5:8–10

Father, You have given me the privilege of being a mother, teaching and helping my children grow into responsible adults. I pray that those You have given me will be acceptable in Your sight. You have spoken in Your Word that we are the light of the world. May we forever walk as children of light and live to bring honor and glory to You. I ask these things in Your precious name. Amen.

AFFECTIONATE

*Be kindly affectionate to one another
with brotherly love, in honor giving
preference to one another.*

—ROMANS 12:10

Lord, You have said in Your Word to be "kindly affectionate with brotherly love" to those around me. Soften my heart and give me a sensitive spirit to my family as well as those I interact with each day. Let my life be a clear reflection of Your love and care for each of us. Help me, O Lord, to look beyond my own selfish desires that I may see the needs and desires of others. In Jesus' name. Amen.

Afraid

Behold, God is my salvation,
I will trust and not be afraid;
For Yah, the Lord, is my strength and song;
He also has become my salvation.

—Isaiah 12:2

Lord, I must confess that I am afraid. Life has given me many challenges, and sometimes I feel so inadequate. Strengthen my heart, and give me a bold spirit to accept the challenges of life. Help me live above my circumstances and rejoice in the power of Your presence. You have told me to trust in You with all my heart (Proverbs 3:5). You alone are my strength and my salvation. Help me rest in this truth today. This I ask in Your precious name. Amen.

ALWAYS

Rejoice in the Lord always.
Again I will say, rejoice!
Let your gentleness be known to all men.
The Lord is at hand.

— PHILIPPIANS 4:4–5

Father, my heart is filled with joy when I recognize that You are always with me. Nothing can separate me from Your love. Today I rejoice in the blessing of Your presence in my life. Help me always to be a blessing to my children and to those in my family. Let me never forget that You are with me always. Open my eyes and heart to Your presence that I may tell others of Your saving grace. In Jesus' name. Amen.

ANGER

"Be angry, and do not sin":
do not let the sun go down on your wrath,
nor give place to the devil.

—Ephesians 4:26–27

Father, I must confess that sometimes I lose my temper. Sometimes, when I am angry, I say words that I shouldn't say to those who love me. Place within my heart the desire to settle all disagreements. Guide my tongue with words that bring peace and contentment to my loved ones. This I ask in Your most holy name. Amen.

ANXIOUS

Be anxious for nothing, but in everything by prayer and supplication, with thanksgiving, let your requests be made known to God; and the peace of God, which surpasses all understanding, will guard your hearts and minds through Christ Jesus.

— PHILIPPIANS 4:6–7

Father, You told us in Your Word to be anxious for nothing, but to come to You in prayer. Open my heart that I might be willing to share with You everything in life that breaks my confidence and takes me away from You. Give me a willing heart to share my life with You, holding nothing back. Lord, I thank You for the promises that You have given me. Protect my heart and mind! In Your name I humbly pray. Amen.

Ask

*Now to Him who is able to do exceedingly
abundantly above all that we ask or think,
according to the power that works in us.*

—EPHESIANS 3:20

Father, my heart aches to know the complete love of Christ. Open my mind and heart that I may see the power of Your glory. Give me a bold spirit to live for You. Place within my heart the love and compassion I so desperately need. Help me run to You each day confessing my shortcomings and seeking Your wisdom and direction for my life. Lord, I ask that Your Spirit guide my life into a deeper relationship with You. Wrap Your arms around me for You are my strength and my salvation. These things I ask in Your holy name. Amen.

ASSURANCE

Let us draw near with a true heart in full
assurance of faith, having our hearts
sprinkled from an evil conscience and our
bodies washed with pure water. Let us hold
fast the confession of our hope without
wavering, for He who promised is faithful.

—HEBREWS 10:22–23

Father, You have invited me to draw near with full assurance of faith. Thank You for that invitation. Fill me with the power of Your presence that You might forever be the center of my hope. Help me, O Lord, to hold fast to my confession and live a life full of Your love without hesitation or wavering. For I know You are faithful and I thank You for Your everlasting love. Bless me that I may bless those You have given me to raise and nurture. In Jesus' name. Amen.

BEAUTY

Do not let your adornment be merely outward—arranging the hair, wearing gold, or putting on fine apparel—rather let it be the hidden person of the heart, with the incorruptible beauty of a gentle and quiet spirit, which is very precious in the sight of God.

—1 PETER 3:3 4

Lord, may the inner beauty that only You can give forever shine through my heart that others may see Your love and grace. Give me a gentle and quiet spirit that glorifies Your presence. Let the beauty of the Holy Spirit shine in my life that everyone will see how precious and important You are to me. Guard my heart from selfishly living to please others with how I look or what I wear. May I be an example to my children that inner beauty comes from You and that it is all You see. This I ask in Your precious name. Amen.

BELIEVE

"Let not your heart be troubled;
you believe in God, believe also in Me.
In My Father's house are many mansions;
if it were not so, I would have told you.
I go to prepare a place for you.
And if I go and prepare a place for you,
I will come again and receive you to Myself;
that where I am, there you may be also."

—JOHN 14:1–3

Lord, help me believe that You are the way, the truth, and the life. My heart yearns for the power of Your presence. Never let me doubt Your love and mercy, but strengthen me to tell others of Your saving grace and never-ending love. May Your Spirit direct my path daily and strengthen my commitment to Your purpose. For without You, I am nothing. But with You, "I can do all things through Christ who strengthens me" (Philippians 4:13). Praise God. In Jesus' name. Amen.

BLESSED

Her children rise up and call her blessed;
Her husband also, and he praises her:
"Many daughters have done well,
But you excel them all."
Charm is deceitful and beauty is passing,
But a woman who fears the Lord, she shall be praised.
Give her of the fruit of her hands,
And let her own works praise her in the gates.

—Proverbs 31:28–31

Father, You have blessed me with the precious gifts of children and a family. May my life reflect Your love and my children know You and Your unconditional love. Guide my thoughts and actions each day, for I am dependent on Your Spirit to guide me with wisdom. Help me be the mother You wish me to be. These things I ask in Your most holy name. Amen.

BLESSING

Blessed be the God and Father of our Lord Jesus Christ, who has blessed us with every spiritual blessing in the heavenly places in Christ, just as He chose us in Him before the foundation of the world, that we should be holy and without blame before Him in love.

—EPHESIANS 1:3–4

Thank You, Father, for the blessings You pour out upon me every day. Help me be a blessing to the loved ones You have given me. Fill my heart and mind with spiritual and logical wisdom that I might always be an example and model for my family. Protect me from anything that would separate me from You and bring dishonor to Your Holy name. Lord, open my eyes that I may bless my children daily. May Your Holy Spirit give me the discernment to be sensitive to all their spiritual and physical needs. May Your blessings forever surround me and keep all of us in the center of Your will. In Jesus' name. Amen.

BURDEN

Cast your burden on the LORD,
And He shall sustain you;
He shall never permit the righteous to be moved.

—PSALM 55:22

Lord, You have invited me through Your Word to cast my burdens on You. I must confess that my heart is heavy and sometimes the burdens of life are too much for me to bear alone. Help me, O Lord, to accept that Your yoke is easy and Your burden is light (Matthew 11:30). Please let me look beyond my challenges and rejoice in the promise of Your presence, for You, O Lord, are ever with me and Your strength will sustain me in all of my circumstances. Praise God in whose name I pray! Amen.

CARE

Therefore humble yourselves under the mighty hand of God, that He may exalt you in due time, casting all your care upon Him, for He cares for you.

—1 PETER 5:6–7

Father, I know that You care for me. Help me to humbly rejoice in the blessings You have given me, as I seek to know You and the power of Your presence today. I will empty myself and give You everything that separates me from You. As a mother, I need Your tender care to encourage and lift me up to be all You wish me to be. Hold me in Your arms and strengthen me for Your purpose. I know You have a plan for me, and I yearn for Your direction. This I humbly pray in Your name. Amen.

CHILDREN

Behold, children are a heritage from the LORD,
The fruit of the womb is a reward.
Like arrows in the hand of a warrior,
So are the children of one's youth.

—PSALM 127:3–4

I praise You, God, for the children You have given me. They truly are a heritage from You. Give me the wisdom to raise each one with the knowledge of a loving Savior. Guide me, O Lord, that my children may know Your saving grace and the power of the resurrection. Protect each one I pray and keep them from harm. Give me the wisdom to make the right choices that will glorify You and develop solid values for the rest of their lives. And Father, let my life be an example of the unconditional love that only You can give. Praise Your Holy name in which I pray. Amen.

CHOSEN

I have chosen the way of truth;
Your judgments I have laid before me.
I cling to Your testimonies;
O Lord, do not put me to shame!
I will run the course of
Your commandments,
For You shall enlarge my heart.

—Psalm 119:30–32

Lord, may Your name forever be praised. I have chosen to live for You and to serve You each day of my life. Help me cling to what is pleasing in Your sight and give me the wisdom to glorify You today and every day. May Your Word come alive in all that I do. Give me the power of Your presence to be the mother You designed me to be and may the way of truth live within my heart always. In Jesus' name. Amen.

CHRIST

*For this reason I bow my knees to the Father
of our Lord Jesus Christ, from whom the whole
family in heaven and earth is named, that He
would grant you, according to the riches of His
glory, to be strengthened with might through His
Spirit in the inner man, that Christ may dwell in
your hearts through faith; that you, being rooted
and grounded in love, may be able to comprehend
with all the saints what is the width and length
and depth and height—to know the love of Christ
which passes knowledge; that you may be filled
with all the fullness of God.*

—EPHESIANS 3:14–19

Father, You have given Your Son, Jesus Christ,
as a sacrifice for my sin. Today I bow my knees in
thanksgiving for the love You have so graciously
demonstrated for me. May You forever dwell in
my heart with Your everlasting love. Fill me with
the power of Your presence through the Holy
Spirit and guide my steps each day to make a
difference in life for Your glory. This I ask in Your
most precious name. Amen.

COMFORT

Blessed be the God and Father of our Lord Jesus Christ, the Father of mercies and God of all comfort, who comforts us in all our tribulation, that we may be able to comfort those who are in any trouble, with the comfort with which we ourselves are comforted by God. For as the sufferings of Christ abound in us, so our consolation also abounds through Christ.

— 2 CORINTHIANS 1:3–5

Lord, my heart is full, for each day You come to me with the comfort of joy and peace that is beyond my understanding. Give me the desire to be a comfort to those who are hurting. Let me be sensitive to anyone who faces the trials and tribulations of life. Help me to reach out with a compassionate heart to share the love of Christ with others. This I ask in Your most holy name. Amen.

COMPASSION

The Lord is gracious and full of compassion,
Slow to anger and great in mercy.
The Lord is good to all,
And His tender mercies are over all His works.

— PSALM 145:8–9

Father, how wonderful it is to know that Your compassion is new every morning. You are forever gracious and slow to anger even when I stumble and fail You in my day-to-day life. Give me a compassionate heart for each one in my family and for those whom I interact with each day. Let my countenance speak volumes of Your never-ending love so that others may know of Your tender mercy and find peace in the arms of our Savior. Praise God in whose name I pray! Amen.

CONFESSION

Seeing then that we have a great High Priest
who has passed through the heavens, Jesus
the Son of God, let us hold fast our confession.
For we do not have a High Priest who cannot
sympathize with our weaknesses, but was in
all points tempted as we are, yet without sin.
Let us therefore come boldly to the throne of
grace, that we may obtain mercy and find
grace to help in time of need.

—HEBREWS 4:14–16

You have promised me in Your Word that if I confess my sins and turn from my wicked ways, that You will hear from heaven and forgive my sins. Help me come boldly to the throne of grace and find mercy in this time of need. Let me praise Your name to each of my loved ones that they may know the never-ending forgiveness and unconditional love that comes to us when we are willing to confess our sins and shortcomings. May God forever be praised. In Jesus' name. Amen.

CONFIDENCE

*Now this is the confidence that we
have in Him, that if we ask anything
according to His will, He hears us. And if we
know that He hears us, whatever we ask,
we know that we have the petitions that
we have asked of Him.*

—1 JOHN 5:14–15

Lord, You have promised that I may come to You with confidence and You will hear my prayer. Let the confidence of Your promise shine through my life in everything that I do. Let my trust in You speak boldly to those whom You have given me to cherish. Let each day begin with assurance in the power of the resurrection and the forgiveness of sin. For it is only through You that we can have the peace that passes all understanding and the reward of everlasting life. In Your most holy name I pray. Amen.

CONTENTMENT

Now godliness with contentment
is great gain.
For we brought nothing into this world,
and it is certain we can carry nothing out.
And having food and clothing,
with these we shall be content.

— I TIMOTHY 6:6–8

Sometimes, Lord, my selfish desires become the major focus in my life, and I find myself wanting more than You have given me. Fill my heart with the peace that passes all understanding. Place within me the desire to be content no matter what my personal circumstances may be, so that my life will be a reflection of Your glory that everyone can see. This I ask in Your holy name. Amen.

COUNSELOR

For unto us a Child is born,
Unto us a Son is given;
And the government will be upon His shoulder.
And His name will be called
Wonderful, Counselor, Mighty God,
Everlasting Father, Prince of Peace.

—ISAIAH 9:6

How comforting it is to know, Lord, that You have given me the Spirit of Jesus Christ to be my Counselor. For I must confess I need Your guiding hand in every area of my life. Help me be the mother I need to be with my children and family. Help me to give them wise and godly counsel through my words and my actions. Give me wisdom and discernment to be a living example of Your unconditional love. Strengthen me daily, Father, that whatever life brings, You will be honored and glorified. This I ask in Your precious name. Amen.

COURAGE

"Be strong and of good courage, do not fear nor be afraid of them; for the LORD your God, He is the One who goes with you. He will not leave you nor forsake you."

— DEUTERONOMY 31:6

Lord, You have asked me in Your Word to "be strong and of good courage," and sometimes I find this very hard. Things in life seem to be more than I can bear. Wrap Your arms around me and hold me close, for I must confess I need the courage that only Your Spirit can give. How wonderful it is to know that You will always go before me, and You will never leave me nor forsake me. Give me the power and courage to live each day in the center of Your presence, and let me sing Your praises forevermore. This I humbly pray in Your name. Amen.

DELIGHT

Delight yourself also in the Lord,
And He shall give you the desires of your heart.
Commit your way to the Lord,
Trust also in Him,
And He shall bring it to pass.

—Psalm 37:4–5

Lord, You are the delight of my life and I thank You for all the things You have given me. Each day, You come to me and fill me with the desires of my heart. You shower me with Your love, and I am forever thankful for the gifts of joy, peace, kindness, gentleness, and self-control. May each of my children see the reflection of Your love in my life daily. I promise to trust in You with all my heart and commit my life to You in every way. Thank You for Your love, mercy, and grace. In Jesus' name. Amen.

DESIRE

"I, Jesus, have sent My angel to testify to you these things in the churches. I am the Root of the Offspring of David, the Bright and Morning Star." And the Spirit and the bride say, "Come!" And let him who hears say, "Come!" And let him who thirsts come. Whoever desires, let him take the water of life freely.

—REVELATION 22:16–17

Father, You are the Bright and Morning Star. How thankful I am that You always reach out with a loving invitation and welcome everyone with open arms. Place within my heart the desire to know You more fully. Let each day bring the peace that only comes from Your presence. May everyone in my family know the joy and love that only You can give. I will praise Your Holy name each and every day, for there is no one like You. Praise God in whose name I pray. Amen.

DISAPPOINTMENT

*And not only that, but we also glory in
tribulations, knowing that tribulation
produces perseverance; and perseverance,
character; and character, hope. Now hope
does not disappoint, because the love of God
has been poured out in our hearts by the
Holy Spirit who was given to us.*

--ROMANS 5:3–5

Life is unfortunately full of disappointments. But You, Lord, have given me a hope
that never changes and a love that will never
fade away. Speak to my heart and give me the
ability to overcome the struggles that are a part
of life. Help me look beyond my own circumstances and see Your purpose for me. I thank
You for the challenges of life that help me walk
closer to You. In Jesus' name. Amen.

ETERNAL LIFE

But now having been set free from sin,
and having become slaves of God,
you have your fruit to holiness,
and the end, everlasting life.
For the wages of sin is death,
but the gift of God is eternal life
in Christ Jesus our Lord.

—ROMANS 6:22–23

Father, I want to shout with joy, for through Your generosity and forgiving Spirit, You have given me eternal life. The sacrifice that Jesus Christ paid for my sins on the cross has opened the doors of heaven to welcome me into Your family. Thank You! May I live each day through the power of Your Spirit. Speak to each one in my family that they too may know the power of Your sacrifice. For You are more wonderful than words can say. In Your mighty name I pray. Amen.

FAITH

*Now faith is the substance of things
hoped for, the evidence of things not seen. . . .
By faith we understand that the worlds were
framed by the word of God, so that the
things which are seen were not made
of things which are visible.*

—Hebrews 11.1, 3

Father, help me live by faith and not by sight. I recognize that faith is not my wishful thinking, but an inward conviction that You will always do what You promise regardless of my circumstances. Through faith, I declare my weakness and at the same time proclaim the absolute trustworthiness of God and Your complete and willing ability to do what I cannot. Help me, Lord, not to have foolish confidence in myself, but to always look to You in every part of my life. For You are always faithful, and I can count on You. Praise God in whose name I pray. Amen.

FAVOR

"Now therefore, listen to me, my children,
For blessed are those who keep my ways.
Hear instruction and be wise,
And do not disdain it.
Blessed is the man who listens to me,
Watching daily at my gates,
Waiting at the posts of my doors.
For whoever finds me finds life,
And obtains favor from the LORD."

—PROVERBS 8:32–35

How wonderful it is to know, Father, that I can listen to You through Your Spirit and wait upon Your presence with joy in my heart. For I have found You, and You have given me Your love, grace, mercy, and favor. Let the joy of my heart spill over to my loved ones. Let the sunshine of Your Spirit shine brightly in all that I do. You have given me more than I can possibly imagine, and I want to live in the center of Your will each and every day. This I ask in Your most precious name. Amen.

FEAR

The LORD is my light and my salvation;
Whom shall I fear?
The LORD is the strength of my life;
Of whom shall I be afraid?
When the wicked came against me
To eat up my flesh, My enemies and foes,
They stumbled and fell,
Though an army may encamp against me,
My heart shall not fear;
Though war may rise against me,
In this I will be confident.

—PSALM 27:1–3

Lord, today I claim Your promise that Your love is greater than any fear I may face in life. I do not need to be afraid of anything when You have given Your Light to guide me. Help me walk in the power of Your Spirit, for Your perfect love casts out all fear. Protect my children from the influence of the evil one. Guide them through Your Spirit to look first and foremost to You. For You are the strength of life, and we have nothing to fear. In Jesus' name. Amen.

FOREVER

Oh, give thanks to the LORD, for He is good!
For His mercy endures forever. . . .
Let those who fear the LORD now say,
"His mercy endures forever."

—PSALM 118:1, 4

Forever is such a beautiful word, and You, Lord, have declared that Your Word, righteousness, truth, mercy, and grace will endure forever, and we will reign with You in eternity. Shower me with Your great mercy that I might proclaim Your Word to the lost. I will tell others of the unconditional love that comes down from the Father who has promised to be with us now and forevermore. In Your most holy name I pray. Amen.

FORGIVENESS

Bless the LORD, O my soul;
And all that is within me, bless His holy name!
Bless the LORD, O my soul,
And forget not all His benefits:
Who forgives all your iniquities,
Who heals all your diseases,
Who redeems your life from destruction,
Who crowns you with lovingkindness and
tender mercies.

— PSALM 103:1–4

Lord, You have forgiven me of my sins and I thank You. Help me remember all Your benefits and be thankful for Your lovingkindness. I recognize that You want every part of my life—body, soul, and spirit. I want to grow closer to You and know the joy that only You can give. May I always reflect Your Spirit of forgiveness to each of my children. Hold me up with Your righteous right hand that I might not stumble. Let me face everything in life knowing that You will be with me. In Jesus' name. Amen.

FREEDOM

Jesus said to those Jews who believed Him,
"If you abide in My word, you are My
disciples indeed. And you shall know the
truth, and the truth shall make you free."

—JOHN 8:31–32

You have said that if I abide in Your word, I shall know the truth, and the truth shall make me free. Open my heart, Lord, that I might have a burning hunger to know You through the power of the Scripture. Give me the wisdom only You can give and place within me the desire to learn more about You. The freedom You give me is precious. Speak to my heart and guide me through Your Spirit that my life will be filled with the freedom of Your love and mercy. In Your most holy name I pray. Amen.

GIFT

Do not be deceived, my beloved brethren.
Every good gift and every perfect gift is
from above, and comes down from the
Father of lights, with whom there is no
variation or shadow of turning.

—JAMES 1:16–17

Father, I must confess that everything I have in life is a wonderful gift from You. You have allowed me to be a mother and to experience the fulfillment that only comes through that gift. You shower me with blessings each day that include family, friends, a place to worship, and the privilege of knowing You. Speak to me daily and help me remember Your unconditional love. Encourage my heart that I may share with others the gift of salvation and boldly proclaim Your saving grace. For there is no one like You. Praise God in whose name I pray. Amen.

GODLINESS

Reject profane and old wives' fables,
and exercise yourself toward godliness.
For bodily exercise profits a little, but
godliness is profitable for all things, having
promise of the life that now is and of that
which is to come. This is a faithful
saying and worthy of all acceptance.

—1 TIMOTHY 4:7–9

Lord, purify my heart and remove from my lips anything that keeps me from glorifying You. May I always seek a life of godliness. You have promised to be with me in all of my challenges, so help me live in such a way as to glorify Your holy name in both word and deed. For You are the Alpha and Omega and without You, I can do nothing. These things I ask in Your name. Amen.

GRACE

For the LORD God is a sun and shield;
The LORD will give grace and glory;
No good thing will He withhold
From those who walk uprightly.

—PSALM 84:11

Father, through Your Word, You bring to light Your saving grace. This is a gift we cannot earn or buy—it is given to each of us freely. Help me live the upright life You describe in Scripture. Be my Sun and my Shield for I need to have the love that only You can give. It is in Your most gracious and holy name I pray. Amen.

GUIDANCE

"However, when He, the Spirit of truth, has come, He will guide you into all truth; for He will not speak on His own authority, but whatever He hears He will speak; and He will tell you things to come. He will glorify Me, for He will take of what is Mine and declare it to you. All things that the Father has are Mine. Therefore I said that He will take of Mine and declare it to you."

—JOHN 16:13–15

Lord, You promise that Your Spirit will come to each of us when we accept You as Lord and Savior. You are our Guide in all truth with authority that only comes from Your Word. Guide me, Lord, as a mother to make good decisions for my children and family. Guard my tongue as I interact with friends and those I come in contact with daily. May Your Spirit always go before me. May You be glorified and lifted up. In Your holy name I pray. Amen.

HAPPY

He who heeds the word wisely will find good,
And whoever trusts in the LORD, happy is he.
The wise in heart will be called prudent,
And sweetness of the lips increases learning.

—PROVERBS 16:20–21

Lord, You make it clear that true happiness comes from You. Speak to me each day. Watch over my thoughts and words and be the center of all that I say and do. The blessings You have showered upon me bring joy, contentment, and happiness. I am thankful for Your kind and tender mercy. Let me be filled with the comfort and power of Your presence. I praise You for Your lovingkindness. In Jesus' name. Amen.

HEAL

"The Spirit of the Lord God is upon Me,
Because the Lord has anointed Me
To preach good tidings to the poor;
He has sent Me to heal the brokenhearted,
To proclaim liberty to the captives,
And the opening of the prison to those who are bound;
To proclaim the acceptable year of the Lord,
And the day of vengeance of our God;
To comfort all who mourn."

—ISAIAH 61:1–2

Lord, You are the great and mighty Healer, Jehovah Rapha. Speak to me and heal the wounds and hurts that burden my heart. Sometimes the responsibilities I have been given are difficult. Heal me and lift me up that I may find joy in You. I need Your strength and the comfort of Your Holy Spirit. Help me glorify Your name and bring praise and honor to You in all situations. For You are more wonderful than words can express. These things I humbly pray in Your name. Amen.

HEART

If you confess with your mouth the Lord Jesus and believe in your heart that God has raised Him from the dead, you will be saved. For with the heart one believes unto righteousness, and with the mouth confession is made unto salvation.

—ROMANS 10:9–10

So many times in Your Word, Father, You speak to me about my heart. Please open my heart and fill me with Your Spirit for You are more precious than silver or gold. You have asked me to trust in You with all my heart and lean not on my own understanding, in all my ways acknowledge You and You will direct my path (Proverbs 3:5–6). May these words come alive in my life today as I share the love You have given me with my family and friends. In Jesus' name. Amen.

HOLY

I beseech you therefore, brethren, by the mercies of God, that you present your bodies a living sacrifice, holy, acceptable to God, which is your reasonable service. And do not be conformed to this world, but be transformed by the renewing of your mind, that you may prove what is that good and acceptable and perfect will of God.

—ROMANS 12:1–2

Lord, I know that You are holy and Your desire is for me to be holy and acceptable in Your sight. Encourage me today as I come to You, laying everything that I have on the altar before You. Sanctify my life and lift me up so that others may see Your reflection in my life. Renew my mind and heart so that I might see You more clearly, for I yearn for the glory of Your presence. This I humbly ask in Your most holy name. Amen.

HOLY SPIRIT

*"If you love Me, keep My commandments.
And I will pray the Father, and He will give
you another Helper, that He may abide with
you forever—the Spirit of truth, whom the
world cannot receive, because it neither sees
Him nor knows Him; but you know Him, for
He dwells with you and will be in you. I will
not leave you orphans; I will come to you."*

—JOHN 14:15–18

What a precious gift You have given me—
Your Holy Spirit abides within me and will be
with me forever. You are the Spirit of Truth
who reveals everything to me. O Lord, help me
to always look to You for wisdom. I am dependent on the power of Your Spirit to guide my
life and bring honor and glory to Your name.
Bless me, oh Lord, that I may in turn bless
those You have allowed me to nurture. In Your
holy name I pray. Amen.

HOPE

That the God of our Lord Jesus Christ, the Father of glory, may give to you the spirit of wisdom and revelation in the knowledge of Him, the eyes of your understanding being enlightened; that you may know what is the hope of His calling, what are the riches of the glory of His inheritance in the saints, and what is the exceeding greatness of His power toward us who believe, according to the working of His mighty power.

—EPHESIANS 1:17–19

How thankful I am that Jesus Christ is my hope and through Him I have life everlasting. I know that the hope of His calling is to live each day in the center of His will. My prayer today is that I might find the Spirit of wisdom, revelation, and knowledge that He has promised so I can know the greatness of His power and share with others the generosity of His love. Thank You for providing that hope to me. In Jesus' name. Amen.

HUMBLE

Therefore submit to God. Resist the devil and he will flee from you. Draw near to God and He will draw near to you. Cleanse your hands, you sinners; and purify your hearts, . . . Humble yourselves in the sight of the Lord, and He will lift you up.

—JAMES 4:7–8, 10

Father, lift me up and guide me to submit to You and resist the devil, for You have promised that he will flee from me. Let me draw near to You each day that I may know You more deeply. Give me a humble spirit to honor You with all that You have given me, for You are my joy and my everything. This I humbly pray in Your most holy name. Amen.

INSTRUCTION

I have taught you in the way of wisdom;
I have led you in right paths.
When you walk, your steps will not be hindered,
And when you run, you will not stumble.
Take firm hold of instruction, do not let go;
Keep her, for she is your life.

—PROVERBS 4:11–13

Lord, I need Your instruction every day. Do not hide Your face from me. Being a mother is complicated and sometimes very challenging. My children and my family need my love and attention. Help me be wise with my responsibilities and uphold me with Your righteous right hand. You are my everything and without You I can do nothing. In Jesus' name I pray. Amen.

INTERCESSION

*Likewise the Spirit also helps in our
weaknesses. For we do not know what we
should pray for as we ought, but the Spirit
Himself makes intercession for us with
groanings which cannot be uttered.
Now He who searches the hearts knows
what the mind of the Spirit is, because
He makes intercession for the saints
according to the will of God.*

—ROMANS 8:26–27

Father, You have given the Holy Spirit who continually makes intercession for me at the throne of grace. As with the Holy Spirit, help me pray continually for each of my children and make intercession on their behalf. I yearn for them to know You and experience the love that only You can give. Lift me up today and fill me with Your presence so that my life as a mother will be all that You wish it to be. These things I ask in Your most precious name. Amen.

JEALOUSY

Set me as a seal upon your heart,
As a seal upon your arm;
For love is as strong as death,
Jealousy as cruel as the grave;
Its flames are flames of fire,
A most vehement flame.

—SONG OF SOLOMON 8:6

Lord, purify my heart. Never let jealousy be a part of my life. Give me the peace that passes all understanding. The love and gifts You have given me are more precious than anything I can imagine. Let my love for others burn more brightly than any selfish thought that I may have. Lord, I confess that I cannot do this without You. Please let Your Spirit give me a generous, loving heart for those around me so that my life will be a mirror of Your unconditional love. This I pray in Your holy name. Amen.

JOY

"If you keep My commandments, you will abide in My love, just as I have kept My Father's commandments and abide in His love. These things I have spoken to you, that My joy may remain in you, and that your joy may be full."

—JOHN 15:10-11

Father, the joy that You give me is so wonderful. Help me live in such a way that Your joy will remain in my heart and life every day. Fill me to overflowing that I may tell everyone of Your never-ending love. I praise You for all the gifts of mercy and grace You so generously give me. Praise God in whose name I pray. Amen.

KINDNESS

Let all bitterness, wrath, anger, clamor, and evil speaking be put away from you, with all malice. And be kind to one another, tenderhearted, forgiving one another, even as God in Christ forgave you.

—EPHESIANS 4:31–32

Lord, let the sunshine of my heart show brightly every day with kindness and gentleness toward each of my loved ones. Help me walk in love and be an imitator of Your loving Spirit. Give me an attitude of generosity that I might not grieve the Holy Spirit. Let me be a shining example of Your love and mercy. Lord, You have blessed me in so many ways, may the life You have given me be a beacon of light that will glorify Your Holy name. It is in Your most precious name I pray. Amen.

LIFE

"Now therefore, listen to me, my children,
For blessed are those who keep my ways.
Hear instruction and be wise,
And do not disdain it.
Blessed is the man who listens to me,
Watching daily at my gates,
Waiting at the posts of my doors.
For whoever finds me finds life,
And obtains favor from the LORD.

— PROVERBS 8:32–35

Father, You are the giver and taker of all things. Speak to my heart and help me gain understanding and forever keep all Your ways. Lord, I confess that wisdom in life comes only from You. Give me the inner desire to know You more intimately and to learn from Your Spirit. Your Word promises that whoever finds You finds life and obtains Your favor. Open my heart that I might continually learn from You and know the power of Your presence. These things I ask in Your holy name. Amen.

LIGHT

*"No one, when he has lit a lamp, puts it in a
secret place or under a basket, but on a
lampstand, that those who come in may see
the light. The lamp of the body is the eye.
Therefore, when your eye is good, your whole
body also is full of light. But when your eye is
bad, your body also is full of darkness.
Therefore take heed that the light which is in
you is not darkness. If then your whole body
is full of light, having no part dark, the whole
body will be full of light, as when the bright
shining of a lamp gives you light."*

—LUKE 11:33–36

Lord, You are the light of my life. My
heart's desire is for that light to shine brightly
so that others may see the love and forgiveness
You have given me. Cleanse me, O Lord, from
any darkness that keeps me from You, for I am
lost without Your tender, loving care. Thank
You for the guidance of your Holy Spirit, who
fills my life daily and renews me to bring honor
to Your Holy name in which I pray. Amen.

LISTEN

Why do you spend money for what is not bread,
And your wages for what does not satisfy?
Listen carefully to Me, and eat what is good,
And let your soul delight itself in abundance.
Incline your ear, and come to Me.
Hear, and your soul shall live;
And I will make an everlasting covenant with you—
The sure mercies of David.

—Isaiah 55:2-3

Lord, sometimes I am so busy with the little things in life that I don't stop and listen to the still, soft voice of Your Spirit. Please forgive me! Direct my life so that You may be lifted up. Help me recognize what is most important. You are the One I long for and live for. Let my soul delight in the power of Your presence. You are more wonderful than words can express. And it is in Your holy name that I pray. Amen.

*But the fruit of the Spirit is love, joy, peace,
longsuffering, kindness, goodness,
faithfulness, gentleness, self-control.
Against such there is no law. And those who
are Christ's have crucified the flesh with its
passions and desires. If we live in the Spirit,
let us also walk in the Spirit.*

—GALATIANS 5:22–25

Lord, I want to live for You. You have
blessed me with children and a special family.
You go before me each day, guiding and direct-
ing my life with gentleness and loving care.
Remove from me anything that does not honor
You. Shower me, I pray, with all the fruits of
the Spirit. May my life be a blessing to those
you have given me the opportunity to touch.
Help me radiate Your love with gentleness,
self-control, kindness, and faithfulness that I
may not only live in the Spirit but also walk in
the Spirit. This I pray in Your name. Amen.

LORD

The LORD is righteous in all His ways,
Gracious in all His works.
The LORD is near to all who call upon Him,
To all who call upon Him in truth.
He will fulfill the desire of those who fear Him;
He also will hear their cry and save them.
The LORD preserves all who love Him,
But all the wicked He will destroy.
My mouth shall speak the praise of the LORD,
And all flesh shall bless His holy name
Forever and ever.

—PSALM 145:17–21

Lord, Your Word speaks boldly of Your righteousness and the beauty of Your grace. I am reminded that You are near for me to call upon with joy in my heart. In everything in my life, You are always there and I will praise You each day, for Your blessings are new every morning. In Jesus' name. Amen.

LOVE

Love suffers long and is kind; love does not envy; love does not parade itself, is not puffed up; does not behave rudely, does not seek its own, is not provoked, thinks no evil; does not rejoice in iniquity, but rejoices in the truth; bears all things, believes all things, hopes all things, endures all things. Love never fails. But whether there are prophecies, they will fail; whether there are tongues, they will cease; whether there is knowledge, it will vanish away.

—1 Corinthians 13:4–8

Lord, love is such a precious, tender word that has such great meaning in my life. To know Your love and the sacrifice of Your Son, Jesus, is the greatest love that I can imagine. Each day, You come to me with a love that seeks no reward, but is unconditional and nonjudgmental. You have given me blessings beyond my wildest dreams. Thank You, Father. Let my life share Your love with those who desperately need You. In Jesus' name. Amen.

MERCY

But God, who is rich in mercy, because of His great love with which He loved us, even when we were dead in trespasses, made us alive together with Christ (by grace you have been saved), and raised us up together, and made us sit together in the heavenly places in Christ Jesus, that in the ages to come He might show the exceeding riches of His grace in His kindness toward us in Christ Jesus. For by grace you have been saved through faith, and that not of yourselves; it is the gift of God.

—EPHESIANS 2:4–8

Lord, through Your tender, loving mercy, You have given me salvation—the greatest gift of all. Through Your goodness, You have chosen to favor me with Your love and life everlasting. Words are not sufficient to express my gratitude for Your lovingkindness. Guide me each day of my life. Help me boast of Your mercy and saving grace that my children will know You and receive You as their personal Savior. I ask all these things in Your precious name. Amen.

MIND

If then you were raised with Christ, seek those things which are above, where Christ is, sitting at the right hand of God. Set your mind on things above, not on things on the earth. For you died, and your life is hidden with Christ in God.

—COLOSSIANS 3:1–3

Lord, clear my thoughts and open my mind that I might see You. Help me dwell on things that will bring glory to You. Renew my mind each day and transform me into the person who wishes to please You through willful obedience to Your Word. Give me the mind of Christ that I might look beyond my own selfish desires and live to please You every moment of every day. For You are more wonderful than words can say. Praise God in whose name I pray. Amen.

MORNING

Sing praise to the LORD, you saints of His,
And give thanks at the remembrance of His holy name.
For His anger is but for a moment,
His favor is for life;
Weeping may endure for a night,
But joy comes in the morning.

—PSALM 30:4–5

Each morning, Lord, I come to You with all of my sorrows and situations in life. And there You are, with Your comforting Spirit that promises even though I may weep with pain and hurt in the night, Your joy is new and alive. You come to me in the morning with strength and reassurance to cope with all of life's challenges. For this, I thank You and praise Your Holy name in which I pray. Amen.

NEW

"I will give you a new heart and put a new spirit within you; I will take the heart of stone out of your flesh and give you a heart of flesh. I will put My Spirit within you and cause you to walk in My statutes, and you will keep My judgments and do them."

—EZEKIEL 36:26–27

Renew my spirit, Lord. Give me a new heart. I find my life as a mother is sometimes stressful. Disappointments come to me, and I feel inadequate for the responsibility You have given me. Give me a new spirit that is eager and willing to do Your will. Help me look beyond the situations I face and to rejoice and praise You for Your tender mercy. For You are with me each and every moment and You will hold me up with Your righteous right hand. Praise God in whose name I pray! Amen.

OBEY

Children, obey your parents in all things, for this is well pleasing to the Lord. . . . And whatever you do, do it heartily, as to the Lord and not to men, knowing that from the Lord you will receive the reward of the inheritance; for you serve the Lord Christ.

—COLOSSIANS 3 . 20 , 23 – 24

Lord, obedience to You is a choice that I must make in life. I pray that each of my children would first be obedient to You and then secondly to me as a mother. Let each step I take glorify Your Holy name. Let me walk in wisdom so that others may see Your saving grace. Lord, I know You have given me special work to do for Your glory. Help me look beyond myself and see what You have carved out for my life. May You forever be praised. It is in Your most holy name that I pray. Amen.

PATIENCE

My brethren, count it all joy when you fall into various trials, knowing that the testing of your faith produces patience. But let patience have its perfect work, that you may be perfect and complete, lacking nothing.

—JAMES 1:2–4

Lord, I find nothing joyful about the trials You have allowed me to face. They seem to come too often. I realize that You often use trials and suffering to test our faith and to help us learn to patiently endure. Give me Your patience with my children that I might be the wise counselor You wish me to be. Lord, You know I need Your wisdom and You promise to give it liberally merely for the asking. I depend on You—never let me doubt Your love and mercy. In Jesus' name. Amen.

PEACE

*Therefore, having been justified by faith,
we have peace with God through our Lord
Jesus Christ, through whom also we have
access by faith into this grace in which we
stand, and rejoice in hope of the glory of
God. . . . Let the peace of God rule in your
hearts, to which also you were called
in one body; and be thankful.*

→ ROMANS 5:1–2; COLOSSIANS 3:15

Father, I am so thankful that by accepting You as my personal Savior I have made peace with You. My life has moved from darkness to light, and I praise Your Holy name. I confess that we are no longer enemies for I am Your beloved child. Help me live in such a way that I might experience the peace of God which passes all understanding. This I humbly pray in Your name. Amen.

PERFECT

You will keep him in perfect peace,
Whose mind is stayed on You,
Because he trusts in You.
Trust in the LORD forever,
For in YAH, the LORD, is everlasting strength.

—ISAIAH 26:3–4

Perfect peace is a gift that only You can give, Lord. My heart burns with desire for Your perfect peace. Let my mind be filled with the power of Your presence. Help me always to trust in You, never doubting Your perfect will, but looking each day to serving You with my whole heart. Strengthen me that I might make a difference for Your glory. This I ask in Your most holy name. Amen.

PRAISE

Praise the LORD!
Praise God in His sanctuary;
Praise Him in His mighty firmament!
Praise Him for His mighty acts;
Praise Him according to His excellent greatness!
Praise Him with the sound of the trumpet;
Praise Him with the lute and harp!
Praise Him with the timbrel and dance;
Praise Him with stringed instruments and flutes!
Praise Him with loud cymbals;
Praise Him with clashing cymbals!
Let everything that has breath praise the LORD.
Praise the LORD!

—PSALM 150

Lord, You tell us to give thanks and to praise You in everything. Through praise I proclaim my dependence on You. Through praise I commit my allegiance and devotion to Christ who gave this life that we might be eternally joined together. With my very breath I will praise You, and I will sing Your praises to everyone. Praise the Lord in whose name I pray! Amen.

PRAYER

*"Call to Me, and I will answer you,
and show you great and mighty
things, which you do not know."*

—JEREMIAH 33:3

Lord, how thankful I am that You invite me to call to You. I recognize that prayer is a vital part of our relationship. I promise to share my most inner thoughts and feelings and to praise and worship You for all that You have done for me. How grateful I am that You have promised to answer me and my requests. I look forward to the great and mighty things that You will show Your servant. I yearn for Your infinite wisdom and understanding so that I might know You and the power of Your resurrection. Praise God in whose name I pray. Amen.

PRIDE

"I, wisdom, dwell with prudence,
And find out knowledge and discretion.
The fear of the LORD is to hate evil;
Pride and arrogance and the evil way
And the perverse mouth I hate.
Counsel is mine, and sound wisdom;
I am understanding, I have strength. . . .
I love those who love me,
And those who seek me diligently will find me."

—PROVERBS 8:12-14, 17

Lord, I recognize that pride has no place in my life. Help me humbly seek to please You with my words and actions. Remove any seed of arrogance from my life. Show me the counsel of Your wisdom that I might have the understanding of Your Word in all that I say and do. Lord, thank You for loving me. Help me seek You with all my heart. You are my everything. And it is in Your most holy name that I pray. Amen.

PURE

Finally, brethren, whatever things are true,
whatever things are noble, whatever things
are just, whatever things are pure, whatever
things are lovely, whatever things are
of good report, if there is any virtue
and if there is anything praiseworthy—
meditate on these things.

— PHILIPPIANS 4:8

Lord, many times I get sidetracked with the situations of life, and I forget to think about the blessings You have given me. Please place within my heart the desire to meditate on You. Remove from my life anything that is not pure, lovely, and virtuous. Help me be content with all that You have given me and live in harmony with all my loved ones. Lead me to be the mother You would have me to be. This I pray in Your holy name. Amen.

PURPOSE

Now He who searches the hearts knows
what the mind of the Spirit is, because He
makes intercession for the saints according
to the will of God. And we know that all
things work together for good to those who
love God, to those who are the called
according to His purpose.

— ROMANS 8:27–28

Lord, search my heart and reveal to me Your purpose for my life. Help me live for You each day. Let Your Spirit guide me so that I might teach each of my children to live for You. I confess that I cannot do what is necessary alone, but with You, Lord, all things are possible. In Jesus' name I pray. Amen.

QUIET

*We urge you . . . that you also aspire to lead
a quiet life, to mind your own business,
and to work with your own hands,
as we commanded you, that you may walk
properly toward those who are outside,
and that you may lack nothing.*

— 1 Thessalonians 4:10–12

Father, sometimes my life is so busy with
family and the responsibilities of life that there
seldom seems to be a quiet time for me to be
with You. Speak to my heart and give me the
desire to step away and spend time alone with
You. Help me look to You each day for reassurance and a sense of peace that only You can
give. My desire is to know You more. May You
forever be praised. In Your holy name I pray.
Amen.

REJOICE

Rejoice in the Lord always.
Again I will say, rejoice!
Let your gentleness be known to all men.
The Lord is at hand.

—PHILIPPIANS 4:4−5

Lord, help me live beyond my circumstances. I must confess there are times when I do not feel like rejoicing. Fill my heart with Your presence, place within me the desire to rejoice in You no matter what is going on in my life. Give me a gentle spirit that brings honor and glory to Your Holy name. You are more wonderful than words can express and Your unconditional love is sufficient for all my needs. Praise God in whose name I pray. Amen.

REST

"Come to Me, all you who labor and
are heavy laden, and I will give you rest.
Take My yoke upon you and learn from Me,
for I am gentle and lowly in heart,
and you will find rest for your souls.
For My yoke is easy and My burden is light."

—MATTHEW 11:28–30

Lord, I accept Your invitation and come to You with an open heart. I want to rest in Your arms and to receive the peace that passes all understanding. Place Your yoke upon me, for I wish to learn everything about You. You are the light of my life, and I am so thankful that I can always come to You for wisdom, strength, and the quiet rest You have promised. In Your most holy name I pray. Amen.

RIGHTEOUS

But let all those rejoice who put their trust in You;
Let them ever shout for joy, because You defend them;
Let those also who love Your name
Be joyful in You.
For You, O Lord, will bless the righteous;
With favor You will surround him as with a shield.

—PSALM 5:11–12

Y ou have promised to bless the righteous, Lord. Place within my heart the willingness to live a righteous life. I need the shield of Your Spirit to surround me each day. I will celebrate Your love and blessings with a pure heart as I live each day to bring honor and glory to Your name. Praise God in whose name I pray. Amen.

SACRIFICE

I beseech you therefore, brethren, by the
mercies of God, that you present your bodies
a living sacrifice, holy, acceptable to God,
which is your reasonable service. And do
not be conformed to this world, but be
transformed by the renewing of your mind,
that you may prove what is that good and
acceptable and perfect will of God.

—ROMANS 12:1–2

Let each day of my life be devoted to spiritual service to You, Lord. Speak to my heart and place within me a desire to do whatever is necessary to be an example for each of my children. You are my everything. Let me be transformed by the renewing of my mind to live each day as a holy sacrifice for Your glory. This I ask in Your most precious name. Amen.

SEEK

Seek the LORD while He may be found,
Call upon Him while He is near.

— ISAIAH 55:6

Father, please help me to never get so wrapped up in myself that I forget to seek You while You may be found. I know the covenant You have made with me is everlasting and no one can take it away from me. I yearn for a closer walk with You and to experience Your loving care. "Let the words of my mouth and the meditation of my heart be acceptable in Your sight, O LORD, my strength and my Redeemer" (Psalm 19:14). In Jesus' name I pray. Amen.

SERVE

*For you, brethren, have been called to
liberty; only do not use liberty as an
opportunity for the flesh, but through love
serve one another. For all the law is fulfilled
in one word, even in this:
"You shall love your neighbor as yourself."*

—GALATIANS 5:13–14

The freedom I have in Christ has been given to me with one purpose: to serve others with joy in my heart and a complete dedication to proclaim the love of Jesus. Lord, place within me a servant's heart, that I might reach out in love to those in need. Never let me forget that it is only through Your loving grace that I am saved. In Your holy name I pray. Amen.

SOUL

The LORD is my shepherd;
I shall not want.
He makes me to lie down in green pastures;
He leads me beside the still waters.
He restores my soul;
He leads me in the paths of righteousness
For His name's sake
Yea, though I walk through the valley
of the shadow of death,
I will fear no evil;
For You are with me;
Your rod and Your staff, they comfort me.

—PSALM 23:1–4

Lord, You are my Shepherd. Each day I look to You to restore my soul and lead me to be righteous, kind, understanding, and a Christian example to those You have given me. Your blessings are new every day, and I thank You for Your grace and mercy in my life. Lift me up so that I may praise Your name forevermore. This I humbly pray in Your name. Amen.

SPIRIT

*Now the Lord is the Spirit; and where the
Spirit of the Lord is, there is liberty. But we
all, with unveiled face, beholding as in a
mirror the glory of the Lord, are being
transformed into the same image from glory
to glory, just as by the Spirit of the Lord.*

— 2 CORINTHIANS 3:17–18

Lord, You have given Your Holy Spirit to live within my heart as a guide for my life. Thank You so much for the freedom I have in You. I can live each day with joy and thankfulness because of You. Bless me that I might bless others with Your love, mercy, and grace. Help me each day to come to You and seek the wisdom of Your Spirit for everything in my life. In Your holy name I pray. Amen.

STRENGTH

God is our refuge and strength,
A very present help in trouble.
Therefore we will not fear,
Even though the earth be removed,
And though the mountains be carried
into the midst of the sea;
Though its waters roar and be troubled,
Though the mountains shake with its swelling. Sélah

—PSALM 46:1–3

Father, You are the strength of my life. In every situation I must face, I know You will be with me. Your Spirit will give me everything that I need to solve the many problems I face. Keep me in the center of Your will that I might not lose sight of Your never-ending love. Lift me up that I will always come to You for guidance and strength in my life. For You are my fortress and mighty God in whose name I pray. Amen.

TENDER

Therefore, as the elect of God,
holy and beloved, put on tender mercies,
kindness, humility, meekness, longsuffering;
bearing with one another,
and forgiving one another,
if anyone has a complaint against another;
even as Christ forgave you,
so you also must do.

—COLOSSIANS 3:12–13

Lord, You have called me to put on tender mercies, kindness, humility, meekness, and longsuffering that I might be an open vessel to those around me who are having a difficult time in life. I want very much to be all that You have asked. Help me to be ever aware of those who need a tender touch of Your love. Make me a beacon of Your forgiving Spirit that I might tell the world of Your saving grace and unconditional love. This I pray in Your most precious name. Amen.

TONGUE

Whoever hides hatred has lying lips,
And whoever spreads slander is a fool.
In the multitude of words sin is not lacking,
But he who restrains his lips is wise.
The tongue of the righteous is choice silver;
The heart of the wicked is worth little.
The lips of the righteous feed many,
But fools die for lack of wisdom.

—PROVERBS 10:18–21

Lord, You have given me a tongue and the ability to speak. Guard my tongue that I might not sin against You and the loved ones You have given me. You have said in Your Word that the "tongue of the righteous is choice silver." May I always be an agent of encouragement reflecting Your love through the words that I speak to others. Help me look beyond my own selfish desires and be sensitive to those who need to be lifted up with a kind word. In Jesus' name I pray. Amen.

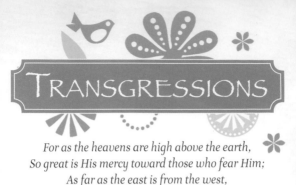

TRANSGRESSIONS

For as the heavens are high above the earth,
So great is His mercy toward those who fear Him;
As far as the east is from the west,
So far has He removed our transgressions from us.

—PSALM 103:11–12

How thankful I am Lord that You remove my sins from me as far as the east is from the west. Because of Your tender mercy, I am free to worship, serve, and live for You. Guard my heart and help me always to keep You in the center of my life. Speak to my children and help them see anything in their lives that will separate them from Your perfect will. Protect them through the power of Your Holy Spirit, so that their lives will be a blessing to others for Your Glory. These things I ask in Your holy name. Amen.

TREASURE

"Do not fear, little flock, for it is your Father's good pleasure to give you the kingdom. Sell what you have and give alms; provide yourselves money bags which do not grow old, a treasure in the heavens that does not fail, where no thief approaches nor moth destroys. For where your treasure is, there your heart will be also."

—Luke 12:32–34

Lord, You are my treasure. Bless me with Your presence, which is more precious than everything else in life. Shower me with Your purpose that I might live each moment with a total commitment to You. I long to know You more and to know the power of the resurrection. Lift me up so that I might praise Your Holy name to those who do not know You. You are the treasure of my life, in whose precious name I pray. Amen.

WISDOM

"Let your heart retain my words;
Keep my commands, and live.
Get wisdom! Get understanding!
Do not forget, nor turn away
from the words of my mouth.
Do not forsake her, and she will preserve you;
Love her, and she will keep you."

—PROVERBS 4:4b–6

The blessing of wisdom is a precious gift that You have given me, Lord. Reveal the wisdom that comes only from Your Spirit. Teach me to be sensitive to Your Word, and give me an understanding of Your plans for my life. Help me share Your wisdom with each of my children, and lead me to influence others for Your glory. In Jesus' name I pray. Amen.

WORTHY

I, therefore, the prisoner of the Lord,
beseech you to walk worthy of the calling
with which you were called,
with all lowliness and gentleness,
with longsuffering, bearing with one another
in love, endeavoring to keep the unity
of the Spirit in the bond of peace.

— EPHESIANS 4:1–3

Lord, help my walk to be worthy of the calling You have given me—looking always to You for guidance, reassurance, and strength. May Your love abound in our family and may we forever have the unity You desire for each of us. May Your Spirit give us the bond of peace that we might show the world Your never-ending love. These things I ask in Your most holy name. Amen.

WORD

In the beginning was the Word, and the Word was with God, and the Word was God. He was in the beginning with God. All things were made through Him, and without Him nothing was made that was made. In Him was life, and the life was the light of men. And the light shines in the darkness, and the darkness did not comprehend it.

—JOHN 1:1–5

Father, You have proclaimed that in the beginning all things began with You, Your Son, and the Word. Through Jesus, everything that we know, have, and are a part of comes from Him. You are the Light that shines brightly in a dark and troubled world. Thank You for creating and loving me and for giving me Your Son so that I may have life everlasting. I praise You for the peace that passes all understanding. Through You I am free to worship with praise and joy in my heart. It is in Your most precious and holy name that I pray. Amen.